FEEDING THE NEW YOU
A Devotional for Spiritual Growth

ISBN 978-0615947365

All Scripture quotations, unless otherwise noted, are taken from
the King James Version of the Bible.

About the Author:

Gewanda J. Parker is the founder and CEO of Hope and Healing Corporation: A corporation with many arms serving and reaching the needs of the marginalized of society locally and abroad to orphanages in Haiti and Africa. In 2003, she started an organization to help young girls and teens suffering with self-esteem and identity issues. Over the years, its changed forms and names and is now affectionately called G-Girls: an acronym used for the different components implemented that foster self-acceptance, self-esteem, mentoring, mothering and sister-ing, of the female gender in all age brackets.

Gewanda is a featured concert soloist and her natural talent in music, and praise and worship has offered her the opportunity to minister and travel singing throughout the US, Canada and Bahamas. Having a true desire to worship through song, coupled with her love of singing, she gathered a group of like-minded others; thus an ensemble group named, Gewanda and Anchored was birthed out of these true authentic worship experiences. They completed their first CD due to release in 2014.

Parker received her Bachelor of Arts degree from Edward Waters College and she holds a Master of Divinity degree from Asbury Theological Seminary. She is embarking upon her Doctoral degree in Pastoral Care and Counseling. Prior to establishing Hope and Healing, G-Girls, and Anchored, she has taught in the public school system as an educator for over 20 years. She was nominated and selected 3 times for the prestigious award for Who's Who Among Americas Teachers; and twice nominated and selected into the Prestigious Cambridge Leadership Award. She was also selected as one of Oprah Winfrey's, educational O Ambassadors for a humanitarian service project for the country of India.

In addition to her educational experience, Gewanda has served as a dynamic ministry leader in the areas of staff pastors, women's leader, administration, worship leader, small group facilitator, missions and pioneering of grass roots ministries. Within the context of sensitive areas, Pastor Johnson has work with multiple multicultural and diversity assemblage of both professionals and laity groups in various settings. Most notable, in 2003, she was asked to speak to the highly Militant

Religious Divides between the Protestants and Catholics in *Belfast, Northern Ireland.* As a facilitator and trainer, she has worked alongside many leadership groups and church leadership teams in the areas of Church Growth and Transformation. Through her experience, she has proven her ability to serve, lead and interact with people of diverse backgrounds. Her initiatives and endeavors, have taken her nationally and internationally to such places as *London England, Duverge, Dominican Republic, (Community Development), Bon Repos, Haiti (Orphanages)* and she spent eight weeks in *Nigeria, Africa (Abuja, Benin, Ewu and Kano)* concentration on cross cultural ministry development.

Using her own life as a catalyst for change, she embodies the message of God's love, healing, transformation and hope. Having been raised in the foster care system, experiencing every form and type of abuse, overcoming stigmas of shame, rejection and unworthiness, she speaks to the transformation of God's healing power and love. She hosted a weekly radio broadcast called Message of Hope, which directed its content to reconciliation and healing of the family, community, spirit, soul, and mind. She has written her autobiography, and is in the process of completing other self-help books that speak to the nature of women's issues, protecting our young and wholeness in its entirety. Gewanda Parker has served as a mentor, trainer, life wholeness coach and spiritual formation guide.

Gewanda Johnson Parker is married to Dr. Elvin J. Parker III and they reside in North Florida.

To contact Gewanda:

www.drejgjparker.org

www.gewanda.com

www.throughgewandaseyes.com

INTRODUCTION

This is a book written to help those who are looking for simple guidelines to help develop spiritual disciplines. The time to digest these concepts can be accomplished within 10 to 30 minute increments. This is not a theological literary approach, rather a practical way to utilize biblical concepts with daily common activities. You may start this booklet at any time and use it seasonally. You will discover that the subject matter for each individual will vary upon life experiences, growth, and development.

Devotionals are good ways to help one focus and be intentional about topical themes or spiritual growth. This devotional is streamlined to individuals who will commit to the process of discipline for 21 or 31 days. Introspective transparency at its deepest level should be desired and sought after throughout the days of journaling. Write it all down and do not hold back. In so doing, you will discover that this approach will yield better results.

If you choose to do this with a group, there are corporate action steps for you to use as a collective body. Using the guided direction in prayer points will reinforce praying on point with a spiritual objective without covering vague topics.

Finally, the mode in which you desire to adjust your physical activities is entirely up to you. The suggested guideline is to help you to be intentional about every part of your life during this period. For those who are accustomed to a life of fasting and self-denial this may be elementary to you so we recommend you consider the Daniel Fast, Partial Fast, Liquid Fast or Complete Fast. Whatever method you choose, do it according to your faith.

May God bless you on your journey throughout this season of consecration and spiritual focusing, growth and discipline. We are in the journey with you in faith, prayer and expectancy of life changing results.

This devotional guide is dedicated to my birth mother,
Alberta L. Johnson aka "Aljo".
and to my foster mother,
Edna Joyce Jackson

A simple daily, spiritual exercise,
Written with you in mind.
"Jauhann"

Period of Self-Denial
21 or 31 Days "CONSECRATION"

SUGGESTED GUIDELINES FOR THIS JOURNEY

1. God will be with you and raise you to a higher level of consecration and discipline. Ask God to help and strengthen you during this time.

2. Drink plenty of water, eat at least 6 times a day, and get good sleep.

3. Be intentional about doing the journaling and action steps.

FOODS YOU MAY EAT:
Brown Rice, Dried Beans, Fruit, Vegetables

LIQUIDS:
Water, 100% fruit juice, 100% vegetable juice, protein drinks. * Juicing is highly recommended

OTHER ITEMS ALLOWED:
Seeds, nuts, olive oil, apple cider vinegar

FOODS TO AVOID:
Meat, White Rice, Fried Foods, Caffeine, Carbonated Beverages. No preservatives or additives, all sugar, sugar substitutes (except stevia) white flour, dairy including butter, yogurt, etc…

SCRIPTURE REFERENCES:
Matt. 6:16-18, 9:14-15, Lk. 18:9-14, Isaiah 58
I Sam. 7:5-6, Ezra 8:21-23, Neh. 9:1-3,
Joel 2:14-16, Jonah 3:5-10, Acts 27:33-37.

Work Exercises for the blank Pages:

Do whatever you want to do, but use the blank pages to be creative and to express yourself. Here are a few example to aid in the process.

1. Write a poem

2. Draw

3. Create a story line with you in it

4. Journal More

5. Practice memorizing the Scripture

6. Write a song

7. Dear God Letter

8. Write a "mock" letter to a real person

9. Reward yourself with affirmations

10. Write out a few personal affirmations.

Other:

Day ONE: THE PRIVILEDGE OF DEDICATION

De 20:5 KJV	De 20:5 Message
And the officers shall speak unto the people, saying, What man is there that hath built a new house, and hath not dedicated it? let him go and return to his house, lest he die in the battle, and another man dedicate it.	*Then let the officers step up and speak to the troops: "Is there a man here who has built a new house but hasn't yet dedicated it? Let him go home right now lest he die in battle and another man dedicate it.*

TODAY WE BEGIN. From this moment turn off all old memories, apprehensions, fears of failure, escape techniques, false unattainable outrageous goals. Settle it NOW! I'm in and I'm in it to the end. No matter how tough it may get or become, no matter what it looks like, despite if or how I may fall off the goal. I will go to the very end of these days of sacrifice.

So then, we now approach it differently. I give all of myself to God. I dedicate this new life to God, I dedicate my appetites to God, I dedicate my temple to God, I dedicate my family to God, I dedicate all relationships to God, I dedicate all of my idiosyncrasies to God, and I move forward in my New Person. In our weaknesses God is strong, in our doubts God is our security, in our challenges God is our victory. God, and God alone, will be the source of our strength, hope, and overcoming.

So, if we are truly dedicated to God and we have turned everything over to God, then we are empty and ready to be filled. Ready to be filed with the newness of all there is in store to come and all there is for us to be.

Today is DEDICATION TIME. We are the new house, the frame is set, but God is the one we will allow to fill the house. POUR IT ALL OUT TODAY. Lay it all on the altar. Do a gully washing of every corner, crevice, and area of your life and walk forward in expectancy of the newness that will come forth.

We are feeding our New Spiritual Person with a totally different kind of diet. We are intentionally shaving away all the fat of sin, slothfulness, doubt, defeat, fear, shame, indecision, hopelessness, depression, perversion, avarice, pride, anger, and bitterness. We are seasoning ourselves with prayer, fasting, study, solitude, and we are embracing the joy of the Lord and the fruit of God's Spirit in our lives. We dedicate ourselves today to God to do a *new* thing in our New Person.

Day ONE: Journal Exercise

Express what the word dedication means to you and how will it look in your life over the next "sacrifice" days?

_____
_____
_____
_____
_____
_____
_____
_____
_____
_____

GOALS TO CONSIDER:

_____
_____
_____
_____
_____
_____

SCRIPTURE TO PONDER:

_____
_____
_____
_____

Day TWO: Feed the NEW YOU an element of SURPRISE!

2 Cor 5:17 KJV	2 Cor 5:17 MESSAGE
Therefore if any man be in Christ, he is a new creature: old things are passed away; behold, all things are become new.	*Now we look inside, and what we see is that anyone united with the Messiah gets a fresh start, is created new. The old life is gone; a new life burgeons! Look at it!*

We take a look at the context of this scripture as we enter in a new spiritual awareness. Old things are passed away. Although we may look the same, situations may appear to be the same, and financial profiles still reflect the same balances, we really are in a **New** day, a **New** season, a **New** dawning of the new Life in Christ. We embark upon this newness by aggressively attacking the challenges we face.

We look forward in faith knowing our God is with us every step of the way. We hold fast to the promises of His sovereignty in our lives and claim as our own that old things are passed away and ALL things are becoming new.

Think on today, this day! What is new in your life? We have to see it, believe it, and move forward into it. See your health taking a new form of wholeness. See your marriage turning and taking a new identity. See your children walking in the fullness of the redemption of Christ. Most importantly, see the new YOU actively engaged with yourself with precision of purpose and fulfillment. Declare it and walk forth in the Newness of Christ's calling in your life.

Today, when you are tempted to revert to the old patterns of living, mindsets, conversations, and routines, deliberately do the opposite. Embody this newness. With your normal daily activities, create an environment of change. Position yourself to live in a new reality. Push beyond the zones of comfort. Be bold in taking a new stand at work. Take a new route home. Sit in a new place at church. Or in the office rearrange your surroundings and work area. Paint the wall, add a flower, hug an elderly person, talk to a child and really listen to his or her never-ending story. Call a neighbor, read a new kind of book, try a new recipe, whatever you decide just be intentional to create newness and taking in a deeper element of change.

Remember it's not the old you doing these things, so when it feels like "this is just not me," you are right. You are transforming into a different person that will be a more refined you. The old person will wither away and the new person will emerge. See yourself in the future and live like you are already there. It's closer than you think and more attainable than you can imagine.

Hard work, discipline, commitment and sacrifice will put you there. It's a New Season, and now you make it a new DAY as you allow a New You to step forward in Christ and doing it God's way. It will be uncomfortable, but take the challenge and go for it. Surprise yourself and introduce the world to the NEW YOU!

PRAYER: *Dear God, help me to see areas of newness in the mundane activities of my life. I desire to explore other areas in my life. I need your help, I'm open for the new experience. Amen.*

<u>Day TWO: Journal Exercise</u>

Today I did (add the new thing you did differently). Write about your feelings. Where did you recognize God giving you a fresh start?

_____
_____
_____
_____
_____
_____
_____
_____
_____
_____

GOALS TO CONSIDER:

_____
_____
_____
_____
_____
_____

SCRIPTURE TO PONDER:

_____
_____
_____
_____

Day THREE: SPRING FORWARD …. THE NEW YOU!

Isa 43:19 KJV	Isa 43:19 MESSAGE
Behold, I will do a new thing; now it shall spring forth; shall ye not know it? I will even make a way in the wilderness, and rivers in the desert.	*Be alert, be present. I'm about to do something brand-new. It's bursting out! Don't you see it? There it is! I'm making a road through the desert, rivers in the badlands.*

Badlands??? Where are the badlands in your life? What is a badland? A badland is anything that does not produce good fruit. It's the wilderness places in our lives. It is the dry places; it's the inhospitable surroundings. It is the harshness of life and everything that doesn't bring the peace of God.

This verse denotes the completion of the action steps taken. It tells of what is to come in the future and it compels one to be in expectancy of the newness that shall spring forth. However, we need to look back at Isaiah 42:9-13 to get the action steps prior to this declaration. *(Read and meditate on the scripture passage.)*

It demands a reaction not merely a response. God promises to the called one that He will take them by their hand making them a light to the people for all to see. This righteous One shall do mighty and great things; open blinded eyes, and bring freedom to the captive. God will rearrange, redesign, and make all things new in dry places - in the badlands.

Here we have a few steps to take. The first step is to SING. Sing unto the Lord. Not only to sing aloud, but cry aloud and make a glorious song from our hearts. Sing a song of praise and adoration unto our God. The twist to this scenario is that sometimes our eyes are blinded and we can't see our way clear. Or our ears are deaf and we hear, but we do not come to a full understanding of the knowledge of Christ in our badlands or in our wilderness times and seasons.

Why would God call the people to sing in such a dry and dreary place? The same reason we are compelled to sing and make our praises known of God's goodness in our lives even through the badlands of the current places.

It's with this expectancy that we look at Isaiah 43:19. This new day will spring forth and there will be newness in our wilderness. As we continuously dedicate our lives to God, there must be change of circumstances and a redefining of our current position.

Revelations 12:11 declares *we overcome by the blood of the lamb and our testimony.* Therefore, we don't always know nor are able to see it all ahead of time, but we can be assured God is making a new path in our lives. God is busy turning our deserts into rivers of living water, flowing in a steady stream of God's promises and blessings. Our job is to just get in the flow. Starting right now, expect new things to begin springing forth in every area.

Day THREE: Journal Exercise

List 3 current BADLANDS and lay them before God. Write out a song or a poem that gives a testimony in advance of how God brought victory into these places. Then turn them into a song of praise and thanksgiving to God.

_____
_____
_____
_____
_____
_____
_____
_____
_____

GOALS TO CONSIDER:

_____
_____
_____
_____
_____
_____

SCRIPTURE TO PONDER:

_____
_____
_____
_____

Day FOUR: CLEAN, TRADE and INSPECT

Gen 35:2 KJV	Gen 35:2 MESSAGE
Then Jacob said unto his household, and to all that were with him, Put away the strange gods that are among you, and be clean, and change your garments:	*Jacob told his family and all those who lived with him, "Throw out all the alien gods which you have, take a good bath and put on clean clothes,*

Time to clean house and do some free trading! Make the trade for the new heart, the new spirit. The most interesting part of this trade off is that when we clean house we have to really clean house. It's comparable to taking out the garbage bag but still allowing the sour stench of rotten food to linger in the bottom of the can. Or rearranging the furniture but failing to vacuum or dust. What about washing the dishes but never sweeping or mopping the floor? It's a half done job and although we've done some cleaning, we've left just enough residue to expose the areas that are still out of order.

Sometimes it calls for another to do a little inspection to help us to see beyond our blind spots. Other times it just takes walking across the floor barefoot for us to feel the grit. So what do we do? God has offered a free trade from the old to the new.

Now, what does house cleaning have to do with newness and trading? It's simple - the clutter stops the flow! It's difficult to see the aliens when they have a place to hide. Many times there are little idols, small gods lurking around in our lives that seem to assimilate into the clutter of life.

When we take the time to clear out clutter we can recognize the foreign agents, the items that are out of place, and we can make the adjustments to allow room for proper alignment. Begin by exposing heart matters, hidden thoughts, inner vows, or addictions. Talk it out, write it out, pray it out, shout it out - just get it out and into the light. Light expels the darkness. Then you can inhale the freedom of the newness that your efforts have brought about. With God it's possible and there is NO SHAME. So, run towards freedom!

Work Exercise: TAKE a field trip around your home (closets, garage, under beds, etc.) INVENTORY! TIME to clear THE CLUTTER. Make the comparison and give yourself an aim to do something daily to make a free trade. Start small, a desk, an area of the room, hang the clothes, scrub the tub, wash the car, pull the weeds.

Day FOUR: Journal Exercise

Tell God all about your idols, then seek support and accountability from a trusted source.

_____
_____
_____
_____
_____
_____
_____
_____
_____
_____
_____

GOALS TO CONSIDER:

_____
_____
_____
_____
_____
_____

SCRIPTURE TO PONDER:

_____
_____
_____
_____

BE CREATIVE

Day FIVE: Feed THE NEW YOU a CLEAR SOUL

Eze 18:31 KJV	Eze 18:31 MESSAGE
Cast away from you all your transgressions, whereby ye have transgressed; and make you a new heart and a new spirit: for why will ye die, O house of Israel?	*Clean house. No more rebellions, please. Get a new heart! Get a new spirit! Why would you choose to die, Israel?*

Yes, it's a little like dying because we have to get rid of the old and make a trade for the new. If you've ever seen anything die or watched a person transition from earthly existence to life eternal, it is a bittersweet exchange that sends us into floods of emotions and discomfort. But in time those same emotions begin to transform into an awkward odd form of acceptance and closure.

Death should not take us into a deep level of dysfunction and insanity. We must allow the circle of life to take its proper slot in our lives as we do some readjustment to the new reality of life.

Memories become more tangible, real, and special. If we are wise, we will begin to create more memories with the living and the here and now. So it is with casting away all of our transgressions and accepting the new heart and spirit God offers.

If we are alive and living, why should we die and decay in the land of the living? What this means is that by allowing wrongdoing, misbehavior, disobedience, indiscretion, offense, transgression, and our rebellion against the truth of God, and allowing Divine standards to take control of our mind, will, emotions, actions, conversations, and relationships brings forth death.

Let the death we experience propel and morph us into a new life of change and wholeness. The question is posed, "why will you die?"

Think and answer this query for yourself. Why die? What do you have to gain? What will you miss out on if you do die? What is your zest for life?

These are soul-searching questions that only you can resolve. You must determine that it's time to make the transition and cross over from the old into the new.

Day FIVE: Journal Exercise

What are your standards? Revisit the old ones to readjust or solidify and establish new ones.

_____

_____

_____

_____

_____

_____

_____

_____

_____

_____

GOALS TO CONSIDER:

_____

_____

_____

_____

_____

_____

SCRIPTURE TO PONDER:

_____

_____

_____

Day SIX: Nourish THE NEW YOU in the form of FAMILY, FRIENDS, and FOES

Eze 11:19 KJV	Eze 11:19 MESSAGE
And I will give them one heart, and I will put a new spirit within you; and I will take the stony heart out of their flesh, and will give them an heart of flesh:	*I'll give you a new heart. I'll put a new spirit in you. I'll cut out your stone heart and replace it with a red-blooded, firm-muscled heart.*
Eze 36:26 KJV	Eze 36:26 MESSAGE
A new heart also will I give you, and a new spirit will I put within you: and I will take away the stony heart out of your flesh, and I will give you a heart of flesh.	*I'll give you a new heart, put a new spirit in you. I'll remove the stone heart from your body and replace it with a heart that's God-willed, not self-willed.*

Let's take note of these two similar verses as we focus on the topic of family, friends, and foe. The first speaks in the third person voice relative to its outward focus with the explanation of what God will do for *them*.

Think who are the "them" in your life. Whose heart is so hard that God needs to perform this spiritual surgery on it? Who are the "them" that need your prayers of intercession? Who are the "them" that need a new heart? Then we read the next line and it switches to first person voice.

Now the attention has been redirected to the personal pronouns "Me," "My," and "I". Why does your heart need a spiritual operation? What area does God need to operate on? What relationship needs to experience the mercy, love, and forgiveness flowing from you? In what area does God need to work in your heart?

Then we skip over several chapters and now this verse is posed in a similar form but it's all in first person voice. If we take the time to read this book, we will see the necessity of needing God to do the heart transplant. Take some time to read and focus on what happens in this book. Locate yourself its pages and cry out to God to prepare you for the surgery of discovery in your relationships.

We will revisit this topic frequently during this devotional. The spiritual heart is a major organ just as is the physical heart is a major organ. In the realm of relationships and our horizontal interactions, our heart must have the right connection vertically with God to walk properly with one another.

Many areas of hurt, betrayal, forgiveness, and rejection that formulate hearts of stone, we must exchange for the heart of flesh. We must remove every stone and repeatedly surrendering our will to God's perfect will and not our own pervasive will.

Day SIX: Journal Exercise

Examine your heart then write a letter to yourself about your heart condition and its current state.

_____

_____

_____

_____

_____

_____

_____

_____

_____

_____

GOALS TO CONSIDER:

_____

_____

_____

_____

_____

_____

SCRIPTURE TO PONDER:

_____

_____

_____

_____

Day SEVEN: FEED the NEW YOU a Gift of Giving

Num 28:26 KJV	Num 28:26 MESSAGE
Also in the day of the firstfruits, when ye bring a new meat offering unto the LORD, after your weeks be out, ye shall have an holy convocation; ye shall do no servile work:	*"On the Day of Firstfruits when you bring an offering of new grain to GOD on your Feast-of-Weeks, gather in holy worship and don't do any regular work.*
Neh 13:12 *Then brought all Judah the tithe of the corn and the new wine and the oil unto the treasuries.*	**Neh 13:12 MESSAGE** *so that all Judah was again bringing in the tithe of grain, wine, and oil to the storerooms.*

IN THIS NEW YEAR, LET US BE INTENTIONAL IN OFFERING TO GOD OUR FIRST FRUITS OF ALL THINGS.

Time   *Talent*

Relationship   *Finances*

Gifts   *Service*

Hopes   *Dreams*

Desires   *Affections*

*Other

Day SEVEN: Journal Exercise

Dear God, what do you want from me? What do you require of me? Show me and help me offer to you my very best and not leftovers.

_____
_____
_____
_____
_____
_____
_____
_____
_____
_____

GOALS TO CONSIDER:

_____
_____
_____
_____
_____
_____

SCRIPTURE TO PONDER:

_____
_____
_____
_____

Day EIGHT: WHERE ARE YOU STUCK?

Duet. 6:5 NKJ	Duet. 6:5 MESSAGE
And thou shalt love the LORD thy God with all thine heart, and with all thy soul, and with all thy might.	*And you shall love the Lord your God with all your [mind and] heart and with your entire being and with all your might.*

Many times our hearts are divided. Our love for God engenders a desire ton have a deeper and more intimate relationship with God. Our desire is overshadowed by something that stops the flow of commitment to a deeper, more passionate, unadulterated love affair with God. There is a person, event, idol, hobby, or fear that hinders our ability to leap off the cliff into the loving arms of the Father.

We are commanded to love God with our whole mind, heart, and entire being. How can we fully obey? What do we need to do to complete this request? It's a personal question we all must ask ourselves. What is the blockage? Maybe it's the fear of the unknown, perhaps it the deep scars of our past and past relationships that causes such a struggle. Or it's just our stubborn pride that coerces us to do things our own way.

God will not withhold any good gift from us, but just like salvation it's something we have the freedom to accept or reject. We have to give up our agenda and accept the invitation of God. Examine today your hindrances and ask The Loving Creator to help you to love with complete resolve.

Day EIGHT: Journal Exercise

Dear God, I really want to love you with all of me, here is where I get stuck………. This is the first line of your letter to God now you complete the rest.

_____
_____
_____
_____
_____
_____
_____
_____
_____
_____

GOALS TO CONSIDER:

_____
_____
_____
_____
_____
_____

SCRIPTURE TO PONDER:

_____
_____
_____
_____

Day NINE: LEAVE and CLEAVE

Duet. 11:22 KJV	Duet. 11:22 MESSAGE
For if ye shall diligently keep all these commandments which I command you, to do them, to love the LORD your God, to walk in all his ways, and to cleave unto him;	*For if you diligently keep all this commandment which I command you to do, to love the Lord your God, to walk in all His ways, and to cleave to Him*

If keeping and following the greatest commandment of loving God with all of our heart, will guarantee the submission and obedience in all the other areas of our life, then what is the downfall of doing this simple thing? DIVISION.

Yes, this mathematical function can shed much light on our inability to LOVE God with all of our hearts and cleave only to God. Yesterday, we dealt with the hindrances that sometimes prevent us from really embracing this love relationship. Today. we want to be a little more introspective into our heart condition.

Where is the sin? Where is the compromise? And where is the struggle? Answer these questions, then we'll more fully understand our dilemma.

Day NINE: Journal Exercise

Help me to see what I need to leave so I can be clean and free to love thee. Listen to your heart and journal everything, person, event, situation that surfaces. Spend some time in prayer over these things.

_____
_____
_____
_____
_____
_____
_____
_____
_____
_____

GOALS TO CONSIDER:

_____
_____
_____
_____
_____
_____

SCRIPTURE TO PONDER:

_____
_____
_____
_____

Day TEN: CIRCUMCISION

Duet. 30:6 KJV	Duet. 30:6 MESSAGE
And the LORD thy God will circumcise thine heart, and the heart of thy seed, to love the LORD thy God with all thine heart, and with all thy soul, that thou mayest live.	*And the Lord your God will circumcise your hearts and the hearts of your descendants, to love the Lord your God with all your [mind and] heart and with all your being, that you may live.*

By definition "circumcise" means to cut around, *since by the rite of circumcision a man was separated from the unclean world and dedicated to God, the word is transferred to denote the extinguishing of lusts and the removal of sins* (Lexicon).

It's clear by this definition that pain is involved. Physically the act of circumcision is a preventative measure to not allow for excess smegma and filth to collect beneath the foreskin, which creates an atmosphere conducive for breeding disease and dysfunction.

Spiritually we should lay before God to allow this same act of cutting away fleshly desires and tendencies to help keep us from the sinful disease of the soul and spiritual dysfunction that will ultimately lead to our spiritual demise. Let me assure you, ultimately it's a good pain that will catapult you and position you for the status of spiritual newness.

Day TEN: Journal Exercise

Help me to heal as I partake in this act of obedience I allow you to do the following in my life. List those areas of necessary healing, ask the Holy Spirit to reveal to you places that are broken and wounded.

_____

_____

_____

_____

_____

_____

_____

_____

_____

GOALS TO CONSIDER:

_____

_____

_____

_____

_____

_____

SCRIPTURE TO PONDER:

_____

_____

_____

_____

Day ELEVEN: Follow and Obey

Jos 22:5 KJV	Jos 22:5 MESSAGE
But take diligent heed to do the commandment and the law, which Moses the servant of the LORD charged you, to love the LORD your God, and to walk in all his ways, and to keep his commandments, and to cleave unto him, and to serve him with all your heart and with all your soul.	*But take diligent heed to do the commandment and the law which Moses the servant of the Lord charged you: to love the Lord your God and to walk in all His ways and to keep His commandments and to cling to and unite with Him and to serve Him with all your heart and soul [your very life].*

There is a popular old hymn entitled, Where You Lead Me, I Will Follow. Then there is another one that says, Trust and Obey. The lyrics continue with… *there is no other way to be happy with Jesus than to trust and obey.* This verse of scripture encompasses all three of our previous days. Loving God, cleaving to God, and today we are compelled to walk in God's ways in obedience.

After Moses had received clear instruction, he gave obedience as a charge to the people. I would say in our time of surrender and sacrifice we cannot take this lightly but completely follow the Shepherd of our soul and obey the instructions He gives to us: Yearly, monthly, daily, hourly, minute by minute, and second by second. When we know better, we do better. We know the higher calling He's beckoning us to attain and embrace now let's be happy in Jesus, trust Him and obey.

<u>Day ELEVEN: Journal Exercise</u>

What does your higher calling look like?

_____

_____

_____

_____

_____

_____

_____

_____

_____

_____

_____

GOALS TO CONSIDER:

_____

_____

_____

_____

_____

_____

SCRIPTURE TO PONDER:

_____

_____

_____

_____

DAY TWELVE: COMPLETE CHANGE

Gen 35:2 NKJV	Gen 35:2 MESSAGE
And Jacob said to his household and to all who were with him, "Put away the foreign gods that are among you, purify yourselves, and change your garments.	*Jacob told his family and all those who lived with him, "Throw out all the alien gods which you have, take a good bath, and put on clean clothes*

Isn't it ironic that Jacob did not just speak directly to himself, rather he included the entire household? The decree was to all, not just one, but to all who were under the same authority, submission, association, and influence.

Now, this is where it gets a little sticky with commitment. Is it okay for me only or do I include my spouse, my children, my friends, my workplace, my business, and the extensions of myself? Yes, the saying is true; no man is an island unto himself. So, if I commit to make the necessary changes in **my** life, shouldn't everything else around me follow suit? Of course! Why is it sticky?

Well, because change doesn't always come easy and sometimes there is a real fight involved. You are no longer the same; thus, this change will have an impact on those around you. Be bold in taking a stand for change and embrace the newness of this new person. *"As for me and my house, we will serve the Lord"*, Joshua declared (Joshua 24:15). Let's follow Jacob's example.

Day TWELVE: Journal Exercise

INVENTORY TIME. List the change that needs to take place in your home, your family, your associations, and your occupation that reflect the holiness of God and the purity of His presence in your life. Then ask God for the wisdom and boldness to proceed accordingly.

_____

_____

_____

_____

_____

_____

_____

_____

GOALS TO CONSIDER:

_____

_____

_____

_____

_____

SCRIPTURE TO PONDER:

_____

_____

_____

_____

DAY THIRTEEN: I AIN'T SCEEEEERED!

Ps 55:19 NKJV	Ps 55:19 MESSAGE
God will hear, and afflict them, Even He who abides from of old – Selah - Because they do not change, Therefore they do not fear God.	*God hears it all, and from his judge's bench puts them in their place. But, set in their ways, they won't change; they pay him no mind.*

Who do you fear?

You are embarking on newness, it's complicated but yet a simple one. Once you can answer the previous question things will be definitive and you'll have the courage to make your stand.

Here's some food for thought as you progress.

Who is more important to you? What do you fear most in this new YOU? In what areas will you have to take a stand as you evolve into the new you? This change will certainly bring discomfort in one area or another. Are you able to handle it? Who will you seek to please? One thing I know to be true is God will be with you. God will help you. God will sustain you. God will encourage you and God will empower you.

Don't be scared, go ahead and move forward in the power and presence of the Holy One

Day THIRTEEN: Journal Exercise

Pour out your heart before God exposing all fears, indecision, doubts, challenges, obstacles that may be hindering you from taking a step forward in your new man, new position, new level in God. Think it's a New You so walk in it, Remember Perfect Love casts out all fear.

_____
_____
_____
_____
_____
_____
_____

GOALS TO CONSIDER:

_____
_____
_____
_____
_____
_____

SCRIPTURE TO PONDER:

_____
_____
_____

Day FOURTEEN: SEPARATE CELEBRATION

Acts 13:2 NKJV	Acts 13:2 MESSAGE
As they ministered to the Lord and fasted, the Holy Spirit said, "Now separate to Me Barnabas and Saul for the work to which I have called them."	*One day as they were worshiping God--they were also fasting as they waited for guidance--the Holy Spirit spoke: "Take Barnabas and Saul and commission them for the work I have called them to do."*

In most cases separation has a drab connotation to it. However, in this case and this one time we should all want to be counted among the ones who were separated. Worshiping God and fasting, so much so, that we are singled out and then put in a position to do the work that God has designed for us to do.

We can't say this is like a prerequisite for greatness in God, but it's more of a lifestyle of greatness and power. Spiritual growth, character development, discipline, self-control and inner fortitude and strength are some by products.

What a grand celebration to know that the purity of my heart has touched the Creator's heart. The killing of my flesh has risen to God's nostrils as a sweet smelling savor. This should draw us nearer to the throne of God and ignite in us a desire and passion to do so much more to please God and to love God without distractions but total abandonment.

Day FOURTEEN: Journal Exercise

*Just express "**YOUR**" self. Have a transparent conversation with God expressing one particular _____ you have yet to come to terms with and how you want to celebrate the conclusion of the matter.*

_____
_____
_____
_____
_____
_____
_____
_____
_____
_____

GOALS TO CONSIDER:

_____
_____
_____
_____
_____
_____

SCRIPTURE TO PONDER:

_____
_____
_____
_____

Day FIFTEEN: Practice brings PERFECTION

Mt 5:48 KJV	Mt 5:48 NAS
Be ye therefore perfect, even as your Father which is in heaven is perfect.	*Therefore you are to be perfect, as your heavenly Father is perfect.*
Lk 6:40	**Lk 6:40**
The disciple is not above his master: but every one that is perfect shall be as his master.	*A pupil is not above his teacher; but everyone, after he has been fully trained, will be like his teacher*

Why practice? Does it really matter? What does this mean in totality? Coupled with this notion of the sharpening of the sword? Why would God be concerned with our level perfection?

We are on a life of progression, upward. The only way is to do what it takes to be the best we possibly can. It's a standard, an expectation of greater. Not a means of enslavement and entrapment of a dysfunctional method of our psyche. It's an invitation to come up higher.

As we spent more time learning about God, We've come to understand that we serve a God of excellence. Nothing God does is a half job, or incomplete. Everything God does is completed with perfection. If we follow God's guidance, then our lives will reflect as much perfection that can be attained.

We have all heard the saying, *"practice makes perfect"* or you go *"from glory to glory."* How do we continue to advance, improve, grow, evolve, and develop? We do this by doing the right things, over and over, improving and honing the skills and gifts God has given us and by subduing our passions and adjusting ourselves. We do it by reevaluating our lives along the way in order that our witness will show evidence of God's transformative power in our lives.

Finally, at the end of one level we continue to practice as we start over by doing it all again in another level. PRACTICE and repetition brings us to PERFECTION. When we begin making the time, researching the sources and taking advantage of the opportunities to grow, we become better in all areas.

This is the practice and these are the keys to spiritual growth. Now we see ourselves in the stages of going from glory to glory and on our way to PERFECTION.

Day FIFTEEN: Practice/Journal Exercise

Do self-examination what area in your life can you apply and produce in a greater measure? Begin today.

_____

_____

_____

_____

_____

_____

_____

_____

_____

_____

GOALS TO CONSIDER:

_____

_____

_____

_____

_____

_____

SCRIPTURE TO PONDER:

_____

_____

_____

_____

Day SIXTEEN: LET us MEDITATE

Ps 77:12	Ps 77:12
I will meditate *also of all thy work, and talk of thy doings.*	*I will* meditate *on all Your work And muse on Your deeds.*
Ps 119:15	**Ps 119:15**
I will meditate *in thy precepts, and have respect unto thy ways.*	*I will* meditate *on Your precepts And regard Your ways.*

Is meditation a little too far out there for our seeker sensitive mentality to embrace doing? Unfortunately, the enemy has polluted the perception of spending time in meditation by tainting and lacing this discipline with New Age, and occult spiritualism. Nevertheless, just as with anything, there is always a counterfeit to the real. God set this as a discipline in the Christian's life and experience.

We are directed to meditate on psalms, hymns, spiritual songs, and to think on those things that are good, lovely, pure, and of good report. The act of renewing our minds daily with the word of God should be incorporated in our daily living so that our thinking, the very thought life, and living patterns can be transformed to the will, purpose, and character of God.

Meditation is a cognitive discipline that will enrich and impact our soul, reshape our habits, alter our moods, create and inspire productivity, and allow clearness of the flow of the spirit. Let us follow the instructions of God to restructure our thought life through this discipline of meditation.

Day SIXTEEN: Journal Practice Exercise

Do it. Meditate. Ponder on God's love, goodness, gentleness towards you etc... Think of a passage of text and digest each part, visualize yourself in the text.

_____
_____
_____
_____
_____
_____
_____
_____
_____
_____

GOALS TO CONSIDER:

_____
_____
_____
_____
_____
_____

SCRIPTURE TO PONDER:

_____
_____
_____
_____

Day SEVENTEEN: Still and Alone with God

La 3:28 KJV *He sitteth alone and keepeth silence, because he hath borne it upon him.*	*La 3:28 NAS* *Let him sit alone and be silent, since He has laid it on him.*
Ps 4:4 Stand in awe, and sin not: commune with your own heart upon your bed, and be still. Selah.	*Ps 4:4 Tremble, and do not sin; Meditate in your heart upon your bed, and be still. Selah.*

There are times when we have to be alone. These times are not times of loneliness in the sense of being left to one's self without any other connection. It is a time to intentionally be alone to connect our inner spirit with the Spirit of God. In essence, we are not alone but totally inhabited by the presence of a loving Creator who desires this time of intimate fellowship.

In solitude we learn to love ourselves, to find our voice, our signature of authenticity. We have the opportunity for a deeper connection with our life and surroundings. We have the opportunity to gain a better sense and identification of what is and what is not. We take a journey inward and find sweet rest in a remote hiding place of succor, away from the noise, away from the distractions, away from the strange voices that call us away from our purpose, our design, pure holiness, and sheer contentment.

Alone is a coveted dwelling place. To be alone with God and to enjoy ourselves in God is a true place of complete satisfaction.

Day SEVENTEEN: Journal Exercise

Create a station of solitary confinement and make time daily to be in solitude and quietness. Turn off the cell phone, radio, TV, internet access, etc... trace what happens in you, with you and with God.

GOALS TO CONSIDER:

SCRIPTURE TO PONDER:

Day EIGHTEEN: IN the VINEYARD

Eph 4:16 NKJ	Eph 4:16 NAS
From whom the whole body fitly joined together and compacted by that which every joint supplieth, according to the effectual working in the measure of every part, maketh increase of the body unto the edifying of itself in love.	*From whom the whole body, being fitted and held together by what every joint supplies, according to the proper working of each individual part, causes the growth of the body for the building up of itself in love*

How do we spend our extra time and moments? Are we sowing seeds in the lives of others? How can a little bit of our time and attention bring joy to another, or relief to another person's situation? What about peace to and in a chaotic situation? What type of service projects can we perform that would help someone else along the way?

Today as you progress through the day look for ways to extend your hand to help, to love, to share to promote, and to serve. Take a backseat to your world and esteem someone else more highly than yourself. You will be surprised at the difference a little act of kindness will make. Then tomorrow look for another way with someone different. The following day, find another person or cause, and then the next day, find yet a different one.

Do you get the picture? Yes, a pattern will have started and now the challenge will be to keep it going.

Day EIGHTEEN: Journal Exercise

How did you see God in your act of service? How were/are you able to pinpoint the presence of God?

_____
_____
_____
_____
_____
_____
_____
_____
_____

GOALS TO CONSIDER:

_____
_____
_____
_____
_____
_____

SCRIPTURE TO PONDER:

_____
_____
_____

DAY NINETEEN: LIFE of FASTING

Mt 6:16 NKJ	Mt 6:16 NAS
Moreover when ye fast, be not, as the hypocrites, of a sad countenance: for they disfigure their faces, that they may appear unto men to fast. Verily I say unto you, They have their reward.	*"Whenever you fast, do not put on a gloomy face as the hypocrites do, for they neglect their appearance so that they will be noticed by men when they are fasting. Truly I say to you, they have their reward in full.*

Did you realize that in the Bible God addresses fasting as **when** and not **if**? This lets us know that fasting is not an option. It is expected of a believer to have this principle and discipline of fasting as a vital and intricate part of life. Not just a once a year isolated event, during the start of the year, or during the Lenten Season. Rather, the expectation is for Christians to **_live_** a "fasted" life. It is a spiritual discipline to be cultivated.

There are many forms of fasting and the life we live should depict many variations of fasting in our week-to-week, month-to-month, year-to-year existence. We should strive to be like the Levites who lived a consecrated life. We should strive to make this year one of developing a life overflowing with fasting and prayer.

Day NINETEEN: Journal Exercise

Do a bible search and look up the men and women who fasted. Jot down the experiences with fasting these men and women had. You will find this activity quite an eye opener.

_____
_____
_____
_____
_____
_____
_____
_____
_____
_____
_____

GOALS TO CONSIDER:

_____
_____
_____
_____
_____
_____

SCRIPTURE TO PONDER:

_____
_____
_____
_____

Day TWENTY: No SWEAT to IMPRESS

2 Co 1:12 KJV	2 Co 1:12 NAS
For our rejoicing is this, the testimony of our conscience, that in simplicity *and godly sincerity, not with fleshly wisdom, but by the grace of God, we have had our conversation in the world, and more abundantly to you-ward.*	*For our proud confidence is this: the testimony of our conscience, that in holiness and godly sincerity, not in fleshly wisdom but in the grace of God, we have conducted ourselves in the world, and especially toward you.*

Earlier we addressed clearing away the clutter, now we look at simplifying the remains. It's simple just, SIMPLIFY and gain a greater understanding of how to have MORE with less. Making things easier for ourselves for the activities we participate in and must do. Simplifying things help shorten the span of time we spend on events and projects with equal amounts of quality given to each without redundancy or wastefulness.

When approaching assignments and projects utilize a straightforward attack method to help alleviate gray areas of confusion. Become more organized so that you can reduce stress and the "hamster wheel" effect. It happens when we feel we are spinning round and round in circles getting nowhere.

Simplicity makes life sweeter, calmer, clearer, and peaceful. Without the extra added bondages and weights, it makes life lighter. When the airways of our minds, hearts, and body are simple we are better able to focus on the things that matter the most.

The Kingdom agenda has an opportunity to rise to the top and life takes on new focus. Really it's a form and level of freedom that allows us to live, work, love, and play on a higher plane. This year when life is overwhelming, watch out for ways of freeing up your time, attention, focus, environment, and mind.

Day TWENTY: Journal Exercise

Let's do it. Simplify. Take anything (item, habit, account) you have *more than one of that serves the same purpose and delete one or more out of your life.*

_____
_____
_____
_____
_____
_____
_____
_____
_____
_____
_____

GOALS TO CONSIDER:

_____
_____
_____
_____
_____
_____

SCRIPTURE TO PONDER:

_____
_____
_____
_____

Day TWENTY-ONE: Just TALK to GOD

1Ki 8:28 KJV *Yet have thou respect unto the* *prayer of thy servant, and to his* *supplication, O LORD my God,* *to hearken unto the cry and to the* *prayer, which thy servant* *prayeth before thee to day:*	*1Ki 8:28 NAS* *"Yet have regard to the prayer* *of Your servant and to his* *supplication, O LORD my God,* *to listen to the cry and to the* *prayer which Your servant* *prays before You today;*

Simply Talking to God. *A young boy was two weeks into a new life of a believer. Prior to giving his life to God, all he knew was gangs and violence. One day while playing basketball with his old friends, a church group on an evangelistic mission came to witness. Just as they began their witnessing techniques, a homeless guy visibly hurt, wounded and in pain, staggered and fell nearby.*

The homeless man began to yell out asking for help. The church group quickly surrounded the man, and began to pray in an unknown language, their language totally puzzled the new Christian and all his friends. Then one member of the church group began to perform a visible exorcism, calling out demons and devils. Another lady took out ointment and rubbed it on the head of the homeless man. The man was in profuse pain and wailed even louder, all along the boy and his friends looked on in shock and disbelief.

Finally, one of his friends looked at him and said, "You gotta help this guy! Ask your God to do something!" Being new to it all and quite nervous and shaken with the entire scene, the young believer agreed the man really needed help. He slowly walked up to the circle of people surrounding the homeless man, kneeled down beside him and asked if he could pray to God on his behalf. The gentleman, at this point, unable to speak violently shook his head with pleading eyes, as if to say YES, PLEASE PRAY FOR ME.

The young boy, said, "Hey God, I don't know what all these other people are doing but would you help this man to feel better and send in an ambulance to take him to the hospital, he really needs your help right now and I'm his mouthpiece?"

Before he could get the words barely out his mouth, two off-duty paramedics were approaching the court to shoot a few hoops. Seeing the crowd, they immediately rushed over. They were able to assess the situation and call for backup. The guy was stabilized and the pain diminished upon their intervention.

The point to this story: **<u>Just talk to God from a pure sincere heart.</u>** God is willing to answer and show up on the scene because you called upon His name with a pure and sincere heart.

Day TWENTY-ONE: Journal Exercise

What does prayer mean to you? How have you possibly complicated this basic avenue of communication? Identify patterns that may distract or prevent you from a life of prayer.

_____

_____

_____

_____

_____

_____

_____

_____

_____

_____

GOALS TO CONSIDER:

_____

_____

_____

_____

_____

_____

SCRIPTURE TO PONDER:

_____

_____

_____

_____

Day TWENTY-TWO through Day TWENTY-EIGHT

Who is this God we praise and worship? This week we are spending time searching, reading, and seeing God in action in the lives of biblical examples and applying them to our own lives. This is somewhat of a trivia to do each day.

Journaling Exercise for each day is to note the name of God and how the name was given. Then we will praise and worship Him for who He is in our lives and who He has been for us.

Names of God to Identify:

Jehovah-Jireh	How does God embody this name?
Jehovah-Rophe	How does God embody this name?
Jehovah-Nissi	How does God embody this name?
Jehovah- Mekaddishkem	How does God embody this name?
Jehovah-Shalom	How does God embody this name?
Jehovah-Roi	How does God embody this name?
Jehovah Tsidkenu	How does God embody this name?
Jehovah Shammah	How does God embody this name?

Scriptures that will help you to find the names of God and identify the characteristics. You are encouraged to read the verse in complete context, story, and chapters.

Psalm 24: 7-10	Psalm 18: 1-3	Psalm 16: 7-11
Psalm 9:1, 2, 7, 11	Psalm 3:3, 4: 5: 1-3	1 Chronicles 29:10-13
Samuel 22:47-50	1 Chronicles 16:23-282	

Day TWENTY-TWO: Journal Exercise

Jehovah-Jireh (God my Provider)

How does God embody this name in your life?

Psalm 24: 7-10   Psalm 18: 1-3   Psalm 16: 7-11

Psalm 9:1, 2, 7, 11   Psalm 3:3, 4: 5: 1-3   1 Chronicles 29:10-13

Samuel 22:47-50   1 Chronicles 16:23-282

SCRIPTURE:

_____

STORY REFLECTION:

_____
_____
_____
_____
_____
_____

PERSONAL EXPERIENCE:

_____
_____
_____
_____
_____
_____

PERSONAL CONFESSION STATEMENT:

_____
_____
_____

Day TWENTY-THREE: Journal Exercise

Jehovah-Rophe (God my Healer)

How does God embody this name in your life?

Psalm 24: 7-10   Psalm 18: 1-3   Psalm 16: 7-11

Psalm 9:1, 2, 7, 11   Psalm 3:3, 4: 5: 1-3   1 Chronicles 29:10-13

Samuel 22:47-50   1 Chronicles 16:23-282

SCRIPTURE:

_____

STORY REFLECTION:

_____
_____
_____
_____
_____
_____

PERSONAL EXPERIENCE:

_____
_____
_____
_____
_____
_____

PERSONAL CONFESSION STATEMENT:

_____
_____
_____

Day TWENTY-FOUR: Journal Exercise

Jehovah-Nissi (The LORD my banner)

How does God embody this name in your life?

Psalm 24: 7-10   Psalm 18: 1-3   Psalm 16: 7-11

Psalm 9:1, 2, 7, 11   Psalm 3:3, 4: 5: 1-3   1 Chronicles 29:10-13

Samuel 22:47-50   1 Chronicles 16:23-282

SCRIPTURE:

_____

STORY REFLECTION:

_____
_____
_____
_____
_____
_____

PERSONAL EXPERIENCE:

_____
_____
_____
_____
_____
_____

PERSONAL CONFESSION STATEMENT:

_____
_____
_____

Day TWENTY-FIVE: Journal Exercise

Jehovah-Mekaddishkem   (God my Sanctifier)

How does God embody this name in your life?

Psalm 24: 7-10   Psalm 18: 1-3   Psalm 16: 7-11

Psalm 9:1, 2, 7, 11   Psalm 3:3, 4: 5: 1-3   1 Chronicles 29:10-13

Samuel 22:47-50   1 Chronicles 16:23-282

SCRIPTURE:

_____

STORY REFLECTION:

_____
_____
_____
_____
_____
_____

PERSONAL EXPERIENCE:

_____
_____
_____
_____
_____
_____

PERSONAL CONFESSION STATEMENT:

_____
_____
_____

Day TWENTY-SIX: Journal Exercise

Jehovah-Shalom (The LORD who brings peace)

How does God embody this name in your life?

Psalm 24: 7-10   Psalm 18: 1-3   Psalm 16: 7-11

Psalm 9:1, 2, 7, 11   Psalm 3:3, 4: 5: 1-3   1 Chronicles 29:10-13

Samuel 22:47-50   1 Chronicles 16:23-282

SCRIPTURE:

_____

STORY REFLECTION:

_____
_____
_____
_____
_____
_____

PERSONAL EXPERIENCE:

_____
_____
_____
_____
_____
_____

PERSONAL CONFESSION STATEMENT:

_____
_____
_____

Day TWENTY-SEVEN: Journal Exercise

Jehovah-Roi (The Lord my Shepherd)

How does God embody this name in your life?

Psalm 24: 7-10   Psalm 18: 1-3   Psalm 16: 7-11

Psalm 9:1, 2, 7, 11   Psalm 3:3, 4: 5: 1-3   1 Chronicles 29:10-13

Samuel 22:47-50   1 Chronicles 16:23-282

SCRIPTURE:

_____

STORY REFLECTION:

_____
_____
_____
_____
_____
_____

PERSONAL EXPERIENCE:

_____
_____
_____
_____
_____
_____

PERSONAL CONFESSION STATEMENT:

_____
_____
_____

Day TWENTY-EIGHT: Journal Exercise

Jehovah-Tsidkenu (The Lord our righteousness)

How does God embody this name in your life?

Psalm 24: 7-10   Psalm 18: 1-3   Psalm 16: 7-11

Psalm 9:1, 2, 7, 11   Psalm 3:3, 4: 5: 1-3   1 Chronicles 29:10-13

Samuel 22:47-50   1 Chronicles 16:23-282

SCRIPTURE:

_____

STORY REFLECTION:

_____
_____
_____
_____
_____
_____

PERSONAL EXPERIENCE:

_____
_____
_____
_____
_____
_____

PERSONAL CONFESSION STATEMENT:

_____
_____
_____

Day TWENTY-NINE: Journal Exercise

Jehovah-Shammah (The Lord is Present)

How does God embody this name in your life?

Psalm 24: 7-10   Psalm 18: 1-3   Psalm 16: 7-11

Psalm 9:1, 2, 7, 11   Psalm 3:3, 4: 5: 1-3   1 Chronicles 29:10-13

Samuel 22:47-50   1 Chronicles 16:23-282

SCRIPTURE:

_____

STORY REFLECTION:

_____
_____
_____
_____
_____
_____

PERSONAL EXPERIENCE:

_____
_____
_____
_____
_____
_____

PERSONAL CONFESSION STATEMENT:

_____
_____
_____

Day THIRTY: Finish Strong

Philippians 3:13-14 KJV	Philippians 3:13-14 NIV
[13] Brethren, I count not myself to have apprehended: but this one thing I do, forgetting those things which are behind, and reaching forth unto those things which are before, [14] I press toward the mark for the prize of the high calling of God in Christ Jesus.	[13] Brothers and sisters, I do not consider myself yet to have taken hold of it. But one thing I do: Forgetting what is behind and straining toward what is ahead, [14] I press on toward the goal to win the prize for which God has called me heavenward in Christ Jesus.

Most of us are familiar with the story of the Tortoise and the Hare or the Little Engine that Could. These childhood staples teach valuables lessons about crossing the finish line. The problem is that we often don't remember these lessons when we are on the track of growing spiritually. You see it's not a race of winning but more of a commitment to stay in the race and run on to see what the end will be.

That last line was a song we use to see back in the AME church. While doing odd jobs at the church, one lady would start singing and then the others would chime in. Sometimes it was heard in what we call a Testimony Service to depict the perseverance of the Christian life.

We've also heard that lesson mirrored in other lyrics or self-help literature. The bottom line is to never quit, don't throw in the towel, don't drop out, keep moving forward until you make it to YOUR finish line. That day will be a glorious day of celebration when we all shall meet God at our appointed time.

During the past 30 days you've been prompted to examine your life in some conventional and unconventional ways. This is the beauty in diversity. God speaks to us in a variety of methods and we each have our tailor-made relationship with God. The one common thread is to make heaven our home but to also have heaven here on earth in a rewarding relationship with God.

It's marvelous and wonderful in His sight. Our Journey on the quest will now take a turn and you will journey without these aids. It is my hope that you will remember them and even revisit them along your journey. These basic practical methods will help you to live well and press forward to the higher calling in Christ Jesus and see what your end will be.

<u>Finish Strong Journal Exercise</u>

What is your game plan? How do you plan to finish the race?

_____

_____

_____

_____

_____

_____

_____

_____

_____

_____

GOALS TO CONSIDER:

_____

_____

_____

_____

_____

_____

SCRIPTURE TO PONDER:

_____

_____

_____

_____

Day THIRTY-ONE: Begin Again

Living a life of prayer, meditation, and discipline is one that we must acquire as we go through our lives of learning how to love God and how to live in total submission unto God.

We would do well to note and remember that our lives are like cars. We must stop and spiritually refuel in order to keep going forward. Do not neglect the maintenance checks along the way. Observing these little routine items help us to operate at peak performance. Spending time with God daily refuels us. Doing focused study and intentional consecration helps us to recalibrate and to pull our spiritual lives back into order.

Today is the end of this Feeding the New You consecration booklet, but it marks the beginning of the New You in spiritual maintenance. For your reading today, select one of your favorite passages and sit with it in quiet reflection. Spend those journaling moments realigning yourself for the next phase. Then write a personal confession you can speak over your spiritual growth journey.

Today, you Begin Again.

Day THIRTY-ONE: Journal Exercise

_____
_____
_____
_____
_____
_____
_____
_____
_____
_____
_____

GOALS TO CONSIDER:

_____
_____
_____
_____
_____
_____

SCRIPTURE TO PONDER:

_____
_____
_____
_____

PERSONAL REFLECTION:

_____
_____
_____
_____
_____
_____
_____
_____

PERSONAL EXPERIENCE:

_____
_____
_____
_____
_____
_____
_____
_____
_____

PERSONAL CONFESSION STATEMENT:

_____
_____
_____
_____
_____
_____

If you choose to use this book with a church, study group or team these are a few suggested prayer points to use as a guided area of prayer focus for group.

CONGREGATIONS:

Corporate Prayer Point:

Pray for Jesus to loosen connective prayer in. **Acts 1:14 Matthew 21:13**

Corporate Prayer Point:

Pray that intercessors will be raised up in your group/church/organization **John 16:23 & 15:16**

Corporate Prayer Point: Pray for signs and wonders. **Acts 2:43**

Corporate Prayer Point Pray for Jesus to be lifted up high in all preaching, praise, and worship gatherings. **Colossians 1:28**

Corporate Prayer Point: Pray for troubled homes to be healed. **Acts 2:46**

Corporate Prayer Point: Pray families (nuclear families and extended) **Ex. 12:21**

LEADERS:

Corporate Prayer Point: Pray for leaders to be blessed with strong understanding of the kingdom of God. **Acts 1:3**

Corporate Prayer Point: Pray for leaders to possess the anointing of God and to be filled with His Spirit. **Acts 1:8, II Peter 1:21**

Corporate Prayer Point: Pray for all leaders to have boldness and courage in handling various kinds of situations. **Acts 4:31**

INDIVIDUALS

Corporate Prayer Point: Pray for strength and endurance. **Psalm 27:14**

Corporate Prayer Point: Pray for strength and endurance. **Psalm 27:14**

Corporate Prayer Point: Pray for humility and repentance. **John 6:44**

Corporate Prayer Point: Pray for the favor of God. **Esther 2:15, Luke 1:30, 2:52**

Corporate Prayer Point: Pray The Beatitudes. **Matthew 5:3-12**

☺

www.ingramcontent.com/pod-product-compliance
Lightning Source LLC
Chambersburg PA
CBHW032141040426
42449CB00005B/354